BUILT FOR SPEED

BOATS

4771

IAN GRAHAM

 Belitha Press

First published in the UK in 1997 by

Belitha Press Limited
London House, Great Eastern Wharf,
Parkgate Road, London SW11 4NQ

Copyright © in this format Belitha Press Ltd 1997
Copyright © Ian Graham 1997

ISBN 1 85561 712 9

British Library Cataloguing in Publication Data
for this book is available from the British Library.

Printed in Hong Kong

Editor: Stephanie Bellwood
Designer: Dave Goodman
Series design: Helen James
Illustrator: Tom Connell
Picture researcher: Diana Morris
Consultants: Stephen Riley, National Maritime Museum
                      Ann Robinson

Picture acknowledgements:
Allsport: 17t Stephen Munday. Banks Sails: 11b. J. Allan Cash: 18b, 22b. Craig Craft Marine UK Ltd: 6t. FastShip Atlantic Inc: 29. Getty Images: 19 Warren Bolster, 23c & 24t Ambrose Greenway, 26. DML Devonport: 13t. Amos Nachoum Photography: 28c. North News & Pictures Newcastle: 16 Raoul Dixon. PPL: 7t Jamie Lawson-Johnston, 21t, 28b Mark Pepper. Quadrant Picture Library: 14t Bryn Williams, 15t. Rex Features: 25 Sipa/Haley, 28t. Frank Spooner Pictures: 21b Kermani/Liaison. Stena Line Ltd: 27c. Sunseeker International Ltd: 9t. TRH: 12b Royal Navy. Wellcraft Marine: 10c.

Words in **bold** are explained in the glossary on pages 30 and 31.

Contents

The quest for speed

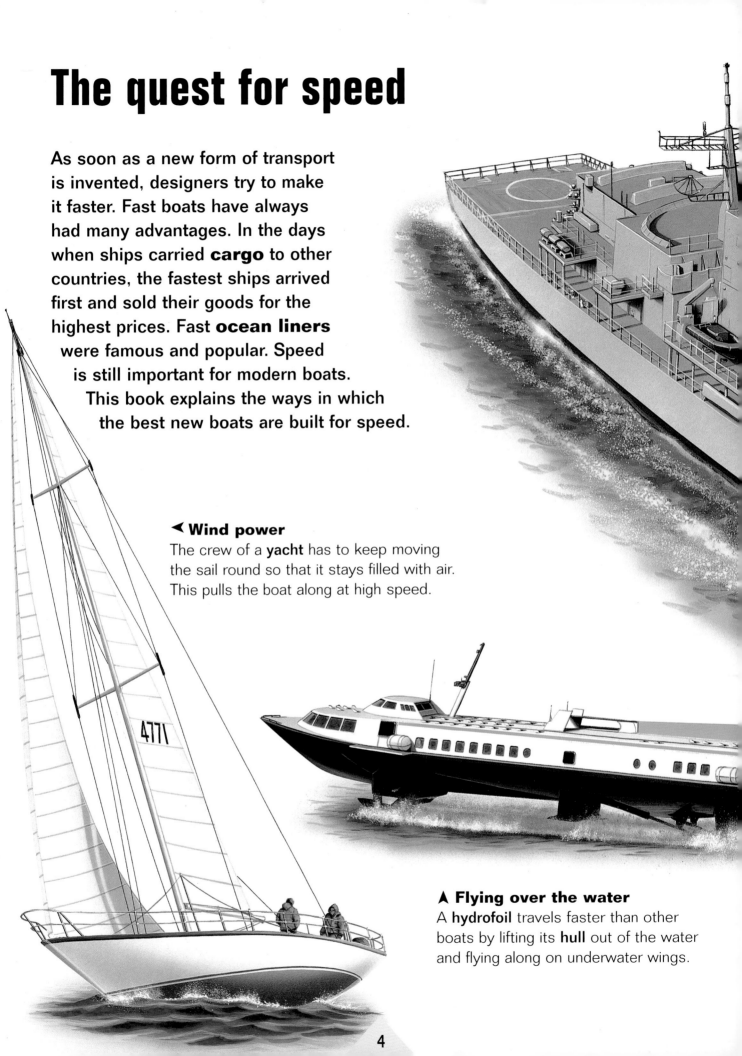

As soon as a new form of transport is invented, designers try to make it faster. Fast boats have always had many advantages. In the days when ships carried **cargo** to other countries, the fastest ships arrived first and sold their goods for the highest prices. Fast **ocean liners** were famous and popular. Speed is still important for modern boats. This book explains the ways in which the best new boats are built for speed.

◀ Wind power
The crew of a **yacht** has to keep moving the sail round so that it stays filled with air. This pulls the boat along at high speed.

4771

▲ Flying over the water
A **hydrofoil** travels faster than other boats by lifting its **hull** out of the water and flying along on underwater wings.

▲ Emergency help
Boats used for search and
rescue work have to race
to where they are needed
as quickly as possible.

◄ Jet ships
Huge warships power through
the water using the same kind
of jet engine as an airliner.

F229

◄ First past the post
Racing boats **skim** the waves with
their engines roaring as they try
to reach the finishing line first.

Designing for speed

Designing a boat for speed means cutting out everything that might slow it down. The lighter a boat is, the faster it travels. The shape of the **hull** is important too. Water pushes against the hull and slows the boat down. This force is called **drag**. Designers make the hull **streamlined** so that it slips through the water easily.

▲ Fun and fashion
Designers look at all sorts of vehicles to find new ideas for powerboats. This fun and stylish new boat is designed to look like a sports car. It can speed over the water at around 80 km/h.

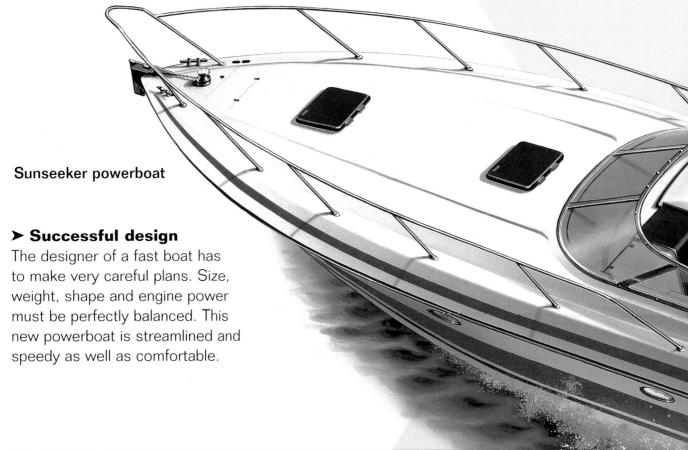

Sunseeker powerboat

➤ Successful design
The designer of a fast boat has to make very careful plans. Size, weight, shape and engine power must be perfectly balanced. This new powerboat is streamlined and speedy as well as comfortable.

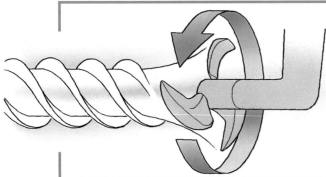

How a propeller works

A powerboat engine is connected to one or more propellers. A propeller has large blades that spin round. As the blades spin, they screw through the water like a corkscrew. This pushes water away and powers the boat forwards.

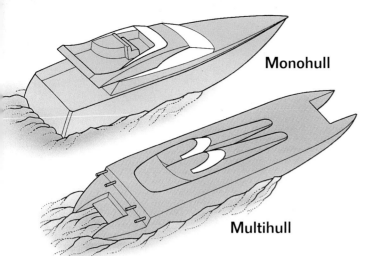

Monohull

Multihull

▲ The fastest hulls

Fast boats are long and slim to cut through the water easily. Two thin hulls slip through the water even better than one hull. A boat with one hull is a **monohull**, and a boat with two hulls is a **multihull**, or a **catamaran**.

▲ Paper boats

Some of the best racing **yachts** have hulls made from paper. The paper is made into a **honeycomb** shape, covered with waterproof material and then stuck to a layer of **carbon fibre**. This makes a strong but lightweight hull.

FAST FACTS

The speed of a boat is not always measured in kilometres per hour. Sometimes it is measured in **knots**. One knot is the same as 1.85 km/h.

On the drawing board

A boat is difficult to plan because designers never know exactly how it will move in the water. The speed and direction of the wind is always changing. A boat **pitches** and rolls as the wind pushes it and waves hit it. The sails or engines also make a difference to the way a boat moves. A new boat is designed very carefully.

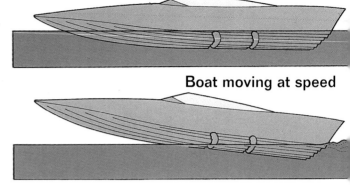

Boat moving slowly

Boat moving at speed

▲ Steps in the hull
Powerboats often have steps or grooves under the **hull**. As the boat moves faster, it rises out of the water. Air is sucked into the grooves. This layer of air between the hull and the water cuts down on **drag**.

➤ Luxury design
This powerboat was designed by computer. It has a **streamlined**, smooth **bow** as well as enough room for a large luxury cabin.

◄ Spinnaker sail
When a **yacht** is moving in the same direction as the wind it can **boost** its speed with an enormous sail called a spinnaker. This is a three-cornered sail that balloons out like a parachute and pulls the yacht along.

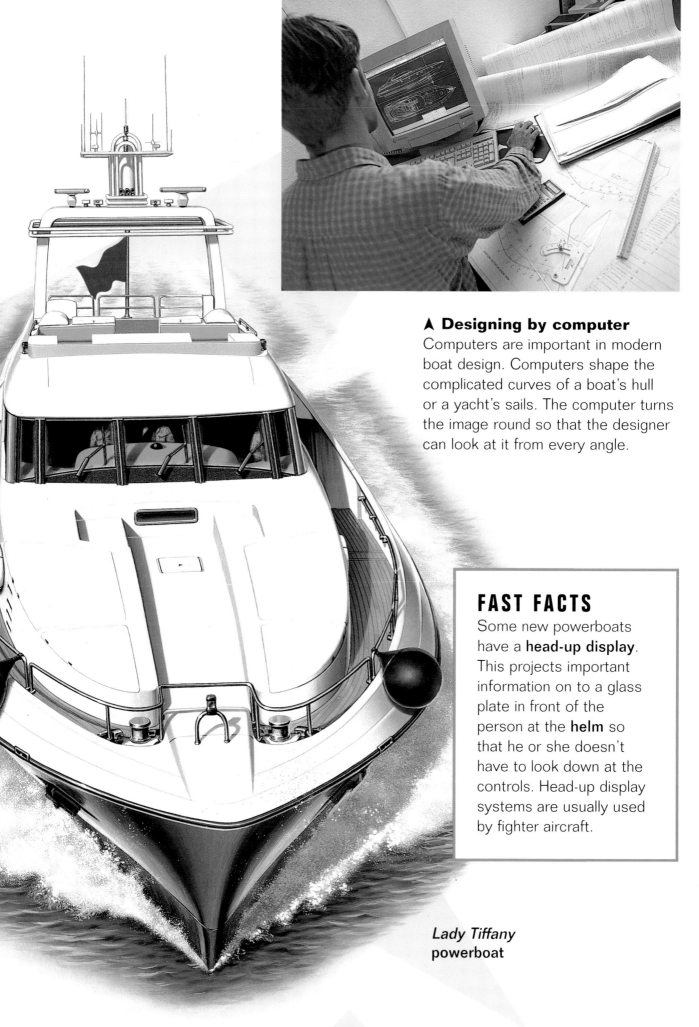

▲ Designing by computer

Computers are important in modern boat design. Computers shape the complicated curves of a boat's hull or a yacht's sails. The computer turns the image round so that the designer can look at it from every angle.

FAST FACTS

Some new powerboats have a **head-up display**. This projects important information on to a glass plate in front of the person at the **helm** so that he or she doesn't have to look down at the controls. Head-up display systems are usually used by fighter aircraft.

Lady Tiffany
powerboat

Will it work?

Boats are tested many times to make sure that they sail properly. Computer pictures show how the boat will move. Small models of the new boat are tested in water tanks. Finally a **prototype** of the boat is built. It is taken out on **sea trials** to make sure that it is safe to use.

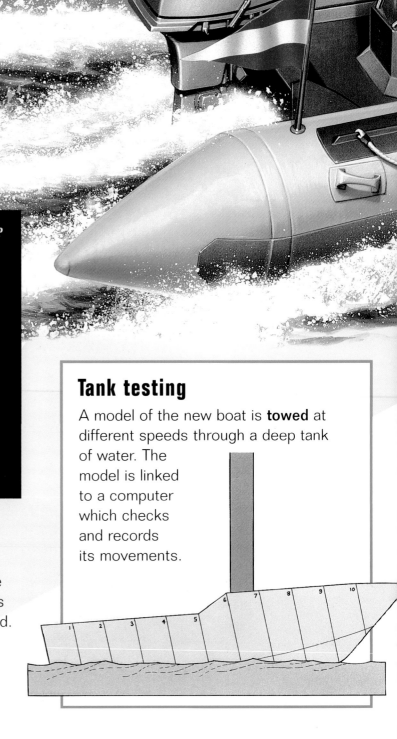

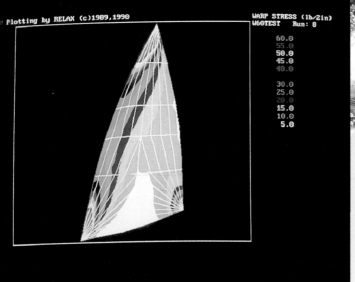

Plotting by RELAX (c)1989,1990

WARP STRESS (lb/2in)
W60TEST   Run: 8

60.0
55.0
50.0
45.0
40.0

30.0
25.0
20.0
15.0
10.0
5.0

▲ Testing by computer
Computers show how a design for a new **hull** or sail will move. This computer image is a sail. It is coloured to show which areas of the sail will stretch most in a strong wind. The designer makes sure these parts are made of a strong material.

Tank testing
A model of the new boat is **towed** at different speeds through a deep tank of water. The model is linked to a computer which checks and records its movements.

Inflatable boat

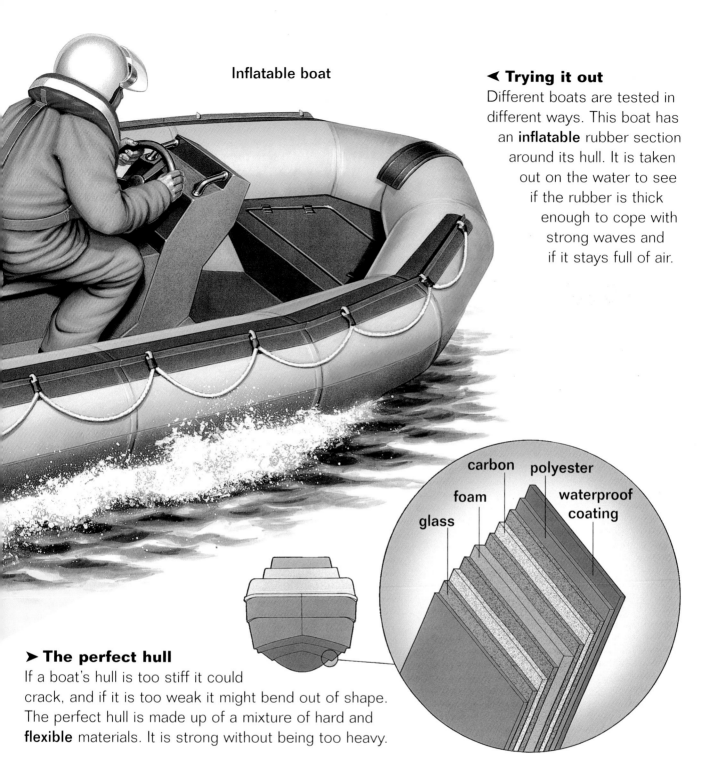

◄ Trying it out

Different boats are tested in different ways. This boat has an **inflatable** rubber section around its hull. It is taken out on the water to see if the rubber is thick enough to cope with strong waves and if it stays full of air.

glass
foam
carbon
polyester
waterproof coating

► The perfect hull

If a boat's hull is too stiff it could crack, and if it is too weak it might bend out of shape. The perfect hull is made up of a mixture of hard and **flexible** materials. It is strong without being too heavy.

◄ Sea trials

A new boat is tested in sea trials by a specially trained crew. The crew test all the boat's controls and check how the engine works at different speeds. Finally the boat is ready to go into service.

Engine power

Fast boats use different types of engines. Small racing boats have petrol engines that work in the same way as car engines. Larger speedboats have bigger and more powerful **diesel engines**. Fast warships are powered by the kind of jet engines used by aircraft. All these types of engines turn propellers that drive the boat through the water.

A personal watercraft

▼ Jet power
Jet engines produce a lot of power. Air and fuel burn inside the engine. The hot gases rush out through a **turbine**. The turbine spins and makes the propeller spin as well.

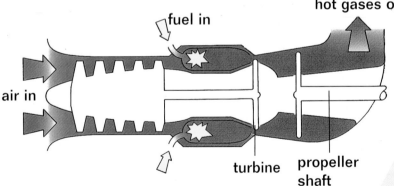

fuel in

hot gases out

air in

turbine

propeller shaft

➤ Nuclear engines
This huge submarine is powered by a **nuclear engine**. Nuclear engines are extremely powerful. They are only used to propel the biggest and heaviest military boats and ships.

▲ Boats without propellers

This military **patrol boat** uses water-jet engines. The engine blasts out jets of water to move the boat along. Boats with water-jet engines can travel in **shallow** water as they do not have propellers that could hit the seabed.

◄ Water bike

A **personal watercraft** is like a motorbike on water. It is powered by a water-jet engine. Water is pumped out at high speed to push the craft forwards.

Engine positions

A boat's engine can be fitted in different positions. Small racing boats have outboard engines which hang on the **stern**, or back, of the boat. Large racing boats have inboard engines which are inside the boat's **hull**. Some boats have an engine which is half in and half out of the boat. It is called a stern drive.

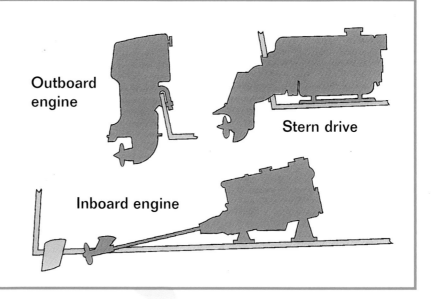

Outboard engine

Stern drive

Inboard engine

Super racers

Powerboat racing is one of the most exciting sports to watch. The racing boats speed along with their engines roaring, **pitching** up and down and leaving tracks of foaming water behind. Powerboats race against other boats of the same size, **hull** shape and engine power. Races can be held on lakes, rivers, and in the sea.

▲ Skimming over water

Hydroplanes are designed for racing along at very high speeds. Their hulls are specially shaped so that they can **skim** over the water at speeds of more than 200 km/h.

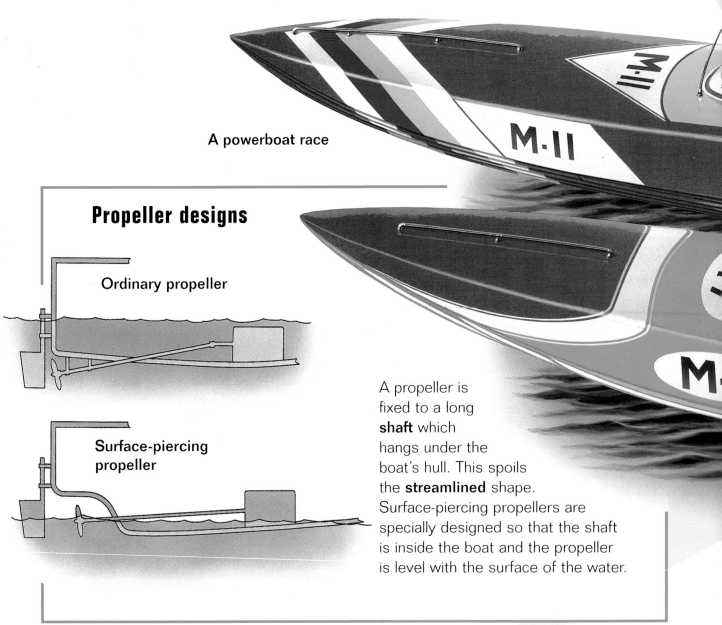

A powerboat race

Propeller designs

Ordinary propeller

Surface-piercing propeller

A propeller is fixed to a long **shaft** which hangs under the boat's hull. This spoils the **streamlined** shape. Surface-piercing propellers are specially designed so that the shaft is inside the boat and the propeller is level with the surface of the water.

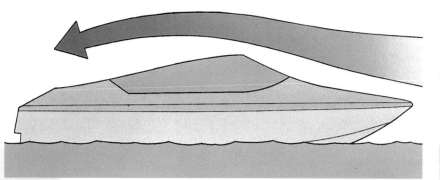

▼ Racing cats

Many racing boats are **catamarans**. They roll from side to side much less than **monohull** boats, which allows them to travel a lot faster.

▲ Streamlining for speed

The streamlined hull of a powerboat cuts down on **drag** from the water. The top half of the boat is also specially shaped. The **cockpit** is low and curved so that air flows easily over the boat without slowing it down.

FAST FACTS

One of the most famous boat races is the American Power Boat Association Gold Cup race. Boats in this race can reach speeds of up to 240 km/h.

Across the ocean

Before the airliner was invented, the only way to travel between Europe and America was by **ocean liner**. Liners raced each other to make the fastest crossing of the Atlantic Ocean. Nowadays fast powerboats compete to see who can cross the Atlantic in the shortest time.

Gentry Eagle
powerboat

▼ Record-breaker
In 1989 an American powerboat called *Gentry Eagle* crossed the Atlantic Ocean in a speedy two days, fourteen hours and seven minutes. This set a new world record.

◄ Giant propellers
An ocean-going ship needs enormous propellers to move it across the water. This huge propeller belongs to a modern **tanker** that weighs 100 000 tonnes. The ship will be used to transport oil.

◀ Racing clippers

The fastest **cargo** sail ships of the nineteenth century were called **clippers**. Modern **yachts** that are based on the old clipper design still race in long-distance events across the ocean.

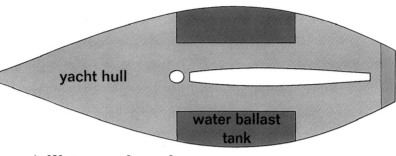

yacht hull

water ballast tank

▲ Water on board

Yachts carry extra weight called **ballast** to stop the boat from being blown over by the wind. Water ballast is pumped into ballast tanks in the hull. It can be let out again when the sea is calm.

Speed over the years

In the early 1800s, **paddle steamers** crossed the Atlantic Ocean in about 18 days. By the 1890s the journey took six days, and in the 1970s the fastest liners could make the whole crossing in just four days.

1800

1890

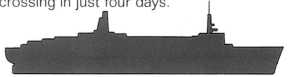

1970

Under sail

The best way to move early boats was to use sails. Now engines are a better way of powering boats, but people still enjoy using sailing boats for fun or for racing. Designers of fast new **yachts** use modern technology to produce the maximum power from the wind.

◄ Racing over ice

Ice yachts run on blades and are the fastest craft with sails. They **accelerate** faster than a Formula 1 racing car and they can whizz along at 230 km/h.

▼ Sailing on dry land

Yachts don't have to sail on water! A sail can be fixed to anything that moves. Sand yachts run on wheels at speeds as fast as 140 km/h when the wind is strong.

A yacht race

Staying upright

The **keel** hangs down under the **hull** to stop the yacht from being blown over. Some keels have a simple shape, but other types, like the winged keel, are shaped to cut down on **drag**.

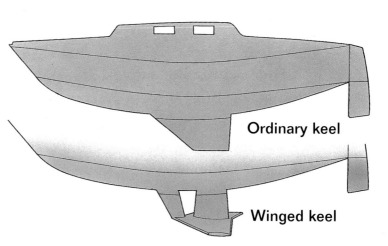

Ordinary keel

Winged keel

➤ Board sailing

Board sailing is one of the fastest ways to **skim** across water. The person on the board uses their body weight to keep the craft balanced. They also move the **polyester** sail round to catch the wind.

FAST FACTS

The fastest sail-powered craft on water is the *Yellow Pages Endeavour*. This strange-looking boat has a tall stiff sail and three tiny hulls. It is called a **trifoiler** and it can sail along at 86 km/h.

Sea cats

The fastest modern yachts and powerboats often have two **hulls** instead of one. These boats are called **catamarans**. The first catamarans were small **yachts**. Nowadays designers also use the catamaran layout for big catamaran ferries. These ferries can cut through the water at very high speeds.

➤ **Amazing sail**
In 1988 the American catamaran *Stars and Stripes* won the famous **America's Cup** yacht racing trophy. The sail looked like an aeroplane wing standing on its end. This unusual new sail was controlled by computers.

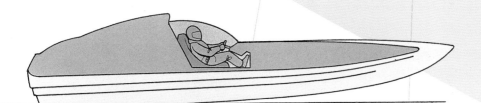

▲ **Inside a racing boat**
Luxury catamaran yachts have a large cabin in the space between the two hulls. Racing catamarans are different. Extra weight slows the boat down, so the crew is squeezed into a tiny space. Racing is not a comfortable sport!

▲ Fast ferries

The world's largest and fastest catamarans are SeaCat ferries. They travel at an average speed of 70 km/h, carrying as many as 450 passengers and 80 cars.

➤ Balancing the catamaran

A catamaran yacht crew stops the boat from being blown over by using their body weight to balance the yacht. They move from one hull to the other as the wind changes direction. Sometimes they have to lean right out over the water.

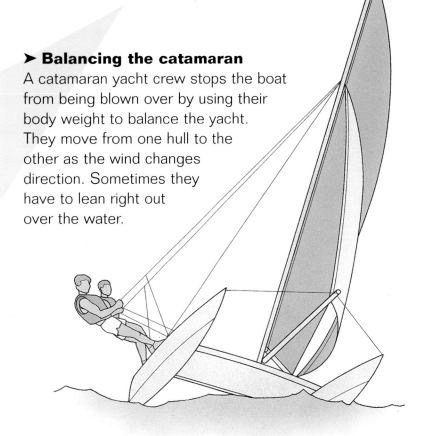

Stars and Stripes
catamaran

▲ Invisible boats

This catamaran is a **stealth ship** called *Sea Shadow*. Its unusual shape stops enemy **radar** from picking up signals that give away its position. This means that it can power along without being spotted.

Wings under water

A boat moves faster if its **hull** is lifted out of the water. A **hydrofoil** boat has underwater wings called foils. The foils are attached to the front and back of the hull by long stilts, or **struts**. When the hydrofoil moves, the underwater wings create lift in the same way as an aircraft wing. The hull lifts out of the water.

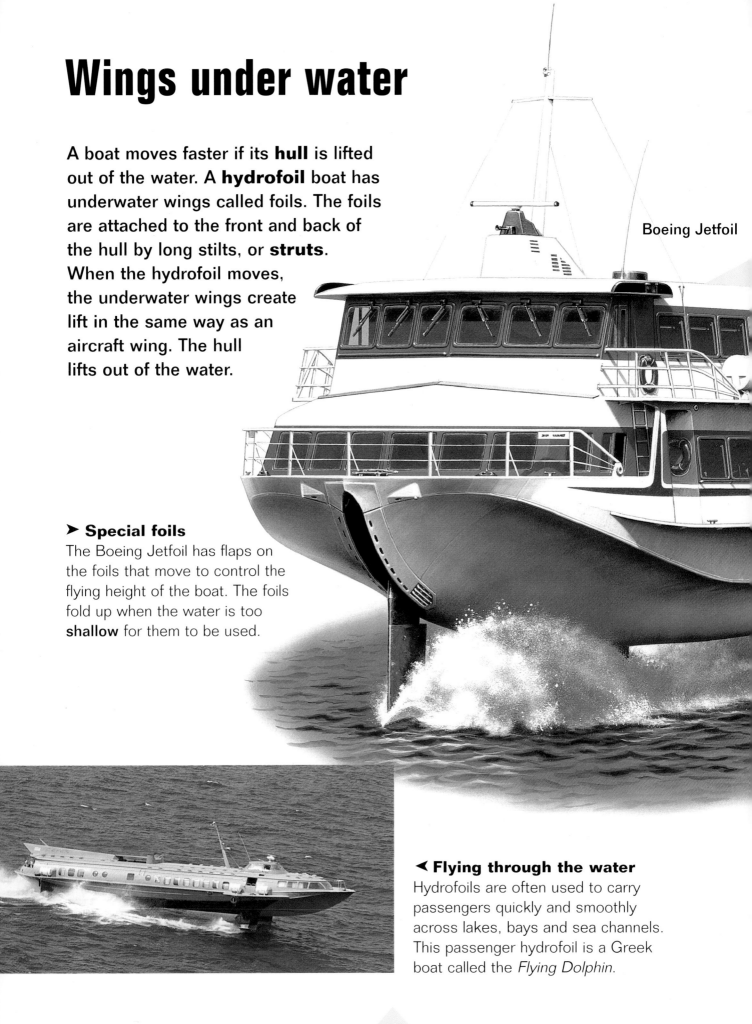

Boeing Jetfoil

➤ Special foils
The Boeing Jetfoil has flaps on the foils that move to control the flying height of the boat. The foils fold up when the water is too **shallow** for them to be used.

◄ Flying through the water
Hydrofoils are often used to carry passengers quickly and smoothly across lakes, bays and sea channels. This passenger hydrofoil is a Greek boat called the *Flying Dolphin*.

Three types of hydrofoils

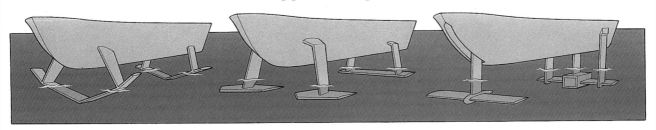

V-shaped foils

Submerged foils

Jetfoil

The underwater wings of hydrofoil boats are not always the same shape. V-shaped foils stick out of the water and help to keep the boat steady.

Submerged foils stay underwater and are moved to change the boat's flying height. A jetfoil has underwater wings and water jets to propel it along.

➤ Staying level

Many hydrofoil ferries have V-shaped foils. The foils keep the boat level and make sure that it does not lift too much.

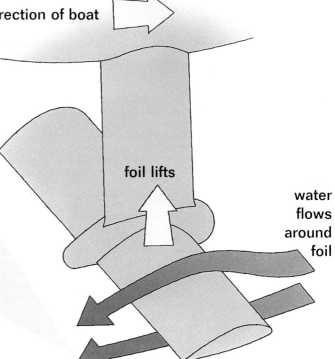

direction of boat

foil lifts

water flows around foil

➤ Sea wings

A foil works in the same way as an aircraft wing. As the foil cuts through the water, its curved shape means that it is sucked upwards by the water flowing around it.

Skimming the waves

A hovercraft is a boat that floats over land and water on top of a cushion of air. Big fans blow air into a rubber skirt under the boat. The boat is not slowed down by **drag**, which means that it is able to travel at very high speeds. The fastest hovercraft in the world belongs to the US navy. This boat can travel at 164 km/h.

▲ The largest hovercraft
The British SRN4 Mark 3 is the largest hovercraft in the world. It weighs 305 tonnes and carries 418 passengers and 60 cars across the English Channel. It travels at a speed of more than 120 km/h.

Racing hovercrafts

▼ Sports skimmers
The invention of the hovercraft led to the exciting new sport of hovercraft racing. Racing hovercrafts are small one-person boats that speed along over land or water.

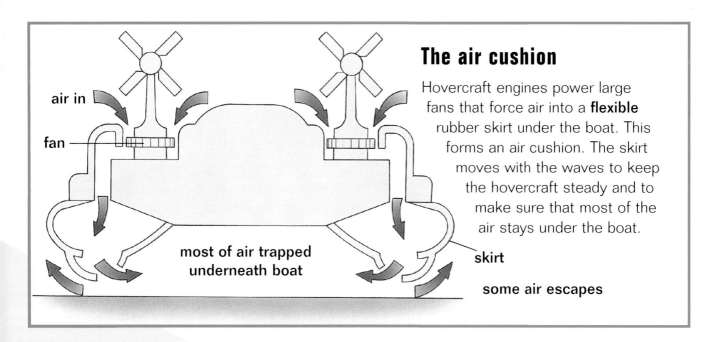

The air cushion

Hovercraft engines power large fans that force air into a **flexible** rubber skirt under the boat. This forms an air cushion. The skirt moves with the waves to keep the hovercraft steady and to make sure that most of the air stays under the boat.

air in

fan

most of air trapped underneath boat

skirt

some air escapes

▼ Moving over land

Hovercrafts are useful because they can travel over land as well as water. Many hovercrafts are used by military forces to carry troops and equipment because they can come on to land to unload.

▼ Winged boat

Airfoil boats also have an air cushion. Short, wide wings on each side of the **hull** trap air underneath. This pushes the boat upwards until the hull rises out of the water. Airfoils can fly smoothly over water at more than 130 km/h.

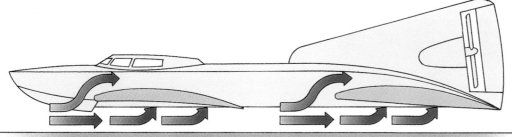

air trapped under wing

Record breakers

The official world water speed record is 511.11 km/h. It was set in 1978 by Kenneth Warby in a **hydroplane** called *Spirit of Australia* on the Blowering Dam Lake in Australia. He had also reached the even higher speed of 555 km/h in test runs. As more powerful engines are developed and new **hull** designs are invented, faster and faster boats will be built.

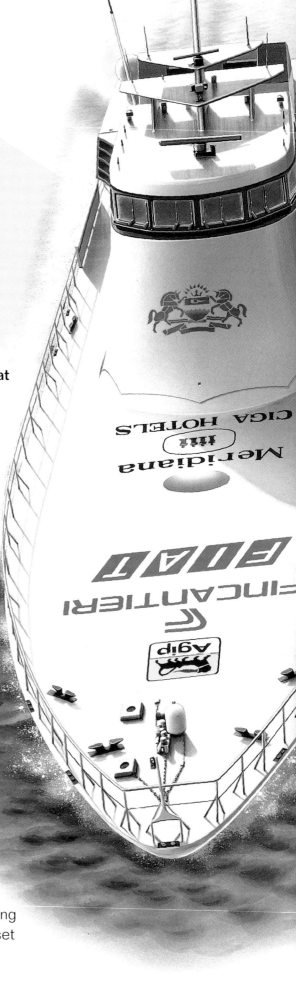

Destriero powerboat

▲ Brilliant Bluebirds
The Englishman Donald Campbell set many speed records on land and water in his blue cars and boats all called *Bluebird*. He was killed in 1967 while trying to beat his own water speed record of 444 km/h in a *Bluebird* boat.

► Across the Atlantic
The record for the fastest Atlantic crossing is two days, ten hours and 35 minutes, set in 1992 by the powerboat *Destriero*.

➤ Fastest ocean liner

SS United States is the fastest passenger ship to cross the Atlantic Ocean. In 1952 she made the crossing in three days, ten hours and 40 minutes.

◄ Speedy ferry

The Stena HSS (High-speed Sea Service) *Explorer* is the fastest car ferry in the world. Four water jets pump out 84 tonnes of water every second, giving the enormous ship a top speed of 80 km/h.

Round the world

The Whitbread Round-the-World Race is the oldest round-the-world **yacht** race. It began in 1973 and it is held every four years. The yachts take about nine months to sail more than 55 000 kilometres. The leading yachts often try to set new speed records during the race.

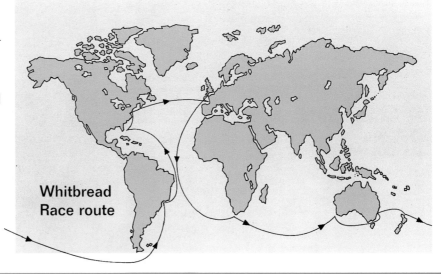

Whitbread Race route

Shaping the future

Even after thousands of years of boat-building, designers are still thinking of new boat designs. Better materials and engines lead to new types of boats. Ideas that failed the first time around can be reworked using new technology such as computers. This means that there will always be ideas for new boats that can travel through or over water faster than ever before.

▼ Boat or plane?

A new boat called a Sea Wing is designed to fly over the surface of the water. As it **accelerates**, its short wings trap a cushion of air underneath that lifts the craft out of the water. It will fly as fast as an aircraft.

▼ Aircraft wings

A **wingsail boat** has a sail which is solid like an aircraft wing. This boat, called the *Walker Planesail*, has three tall stiff wings that are moved by computer. The *Planesail* travels a lot faster than boats with cloth sails.

▲ Jet submarine

Deep Flight is a new type of submarine. Ordinary submarines control their depth by letting water in and out of **ballast** tanks. *Deep Flight* works more like a jet fighter. It uses its wings, tail and **fins** to control its movements. It flies through the water.

28

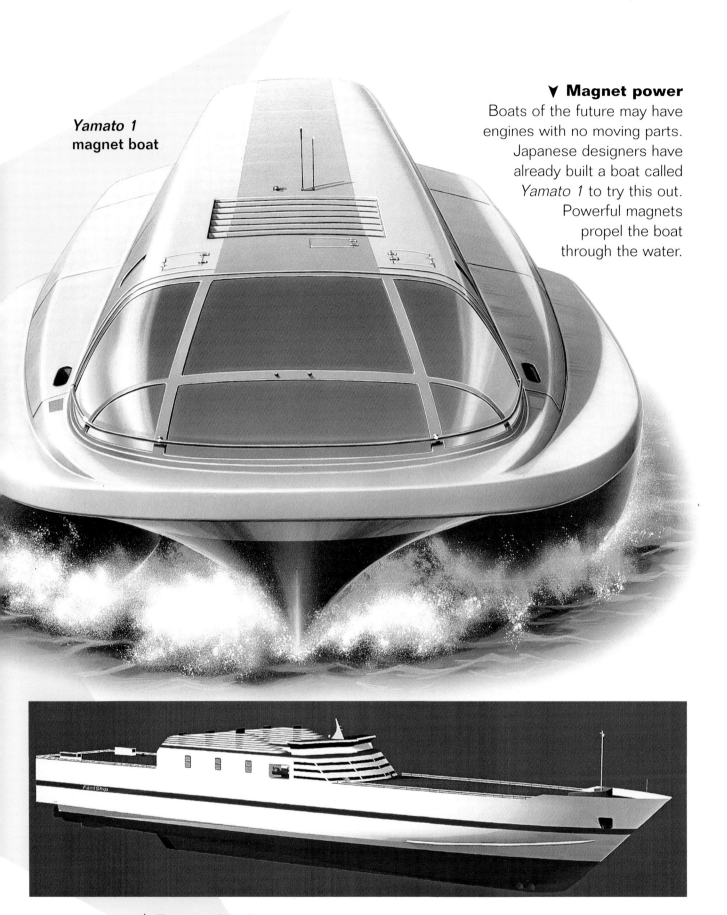

Yamato 1
magnet boat

▼ **Magnet power**
Boats of the future may have
engines with no moving parts.
Japanese designers have
already built a boat called
Yamato 1 to try this out.
Powerful magnets
propel the boat
through the water.

▲ **Extra wide boat**
A new US boat design called FastShip is unusual because its **stern** is
wide and hollow. Ordinary boats have a long thin stern which sinks down
in the water, but FastShip lifts up at the back. This will let it travel faster.

Glossary

accelerate
To move faster and faster.

America's Cup
The most famous yacht-racing trophy in the world. Crews from many different countries take part. There are seven races in the competition, and the yacht that wins the most races is the overall winner.

ballast
Extra weight carried by light boats such as yachts. This weight keeps the boat steady in the water. Ballast can be anything heavy, such as iron, lead, concrete or water.

boost
To increase speed by adding extra fuel or power.

bow
The front of a boat or a ship. The bow is smooth and slim and ends in a point. This shape helps the boat to cut through the water easily.

carbon fibre
A material made of long threads of carbon, which is a very strong black substance. The threads are covered in plastic.

cargo
Goods carried by a boat or any other vehicle.

catamaran
A boat with two hulls. A catamaran can also be called a multihull.

clipper
A fast ship with large sails. Clippers were the fastest cargo ships of the nineteenth century. They were called clippers because they 'clipped', or cut, days off the time other cargo ships took to cross the ocean.

cockpit
The small space in a racing boat or in any other racing vehicle where the crew sits. The cockpit is low and streamlined, and the cockpit cover is clear to give the crew a good all-round view.

diesel engine
A type of engine used to power big, heavy vehicles.

drag
Drag, or water resistance, is the force that pushes against a boat as it moves through the water. This slows the boat down.

fins
Small wings sticking out from the back of an underwater craft. The fins keep the craft steady and help to control the way it moves.

flexible
A flexible material bends easily without breaking.

head-up display
A system that displays important information about a boat's speed and position on the windscreen in front of the driver. The driver can then concentrate on steering the boat without having to look down at the controls all the time.

helm
The steering wheel and other controls. The driver stands at the helm to steer the boat.

honeycomb
The shape of a material that is specially layered and built up so that it is full of holes. This makes it thick and strong but not too heavy.

hull
The main body of a boat that sits in the water.

hydrofoil
A type of boat that has underwater wings. The wings, or foils, are fixed to long stilts underneath the hull. As the boat speeds along, the wings lift the hull out of the water.

hydroplane
A powerboat with a specially shaped hull that lifts out of the water when the boat starts to move quickly. Hydroplanes can skim across the water at high speeds.

inflatable
Filled with air. Inflatable boats are small craft with an air-filled rubber ring around the hull. They are used for fun and emergency rescue work.

keel
Part of a yacht's hull that hangs down in the water. It is heavy to stop the boat from being blown over in strong winds.

knot
A measurement used to describe the speed of boats and ships. One knot is the same speed as 1.85 km/h.

monohull
A boat with one hull.

multihull
A boat with more than one hull. A boat with two hulls can also be called a catamaran. A boat with three hulls is also called a trimaran.

nuclear engine
This type of engine uses nuclear energy to drive it along. Nuclear power comes from a chemical reaction.

ocean liner
A large ship used to transport passengers across the ocean. Nowadays big comfortable liners are used for long, luxury cruises across the ocean.

paddle steamer
An old-fashioned type of ship. It has one or two large wheels with flat, wide blades. An engine powers the wheels, which turn to push the ship through the water.

patrol boat
A military boat that circles a certain area to make security checks or to keep watch on something.

personal watercraft
A kind of motorbike on water, used in watersports. It is often called a PWC for short.

pitch
To move up and down. A boat pitches up and down in a rough sea.

polyester
A thin plastic material. It is used to make sails because it does not tear easily.

prototype
The first full-sized boat that is built using a new design. The prototype is tested to make sure that it works properly. Then many more boats are built and sold to the public or put into service.

radar
Equipment that can pick up signals from objects that are too far away to be seen, and work out their exact position. The results are shown on a radar screen, which looks like a computer screen.

sea trial
A test carried out at sea to check that every part of a new boat is in working order.

shaft
A long pole that can be used to connect a boat propeller to the engine. The engine turns the shaft, which then turns the propeller.

shallow
Water that is not deep.

skim
To race quickly and lightly over the water, hardly touching the surface.

stealth ship
A military boat that is specially designed to travel across an ocean without being seen on enemy radar screens. Stealth ships are used for secret missions or surprise attacks.

stern
The back of a boat or a ship. The stern is always much wider than the front, or the bow, of the boat.

streamlined
A smooth and slim shape. The hulls of fast boats are streamlined so that they slip through the water easily.

strut
A stiff rod that holds part of a boat in place. Hydrofoils have long struts underneath the hull that hold the wings in place under the water.

tanker
A ship that is designed to carry large amounts of liquid such as oil.

tow
To pull something along on a rope or a wire.

trifoiler
A boat with three hulls that are so small they are more like floats. The *Yellow Pages Endeavour* boat is the best example of a trifoiler.

turbine
Part of a jet engine. A turbine is a flat, round plate with blades fixed around the edge. Hot gases rush through the engine and make the turbine spin round. The turbine makes the propeller turn.

wingsail boat
A new kind of boat with three stiff sails that look like aircraft wings standing straight up. The sails are controlled by a computer on board the boat. They work much better than ordinary cloth sails.

yacht
A boat that uses sail power. Yachts are used for racing and for fun.

Index